Demystifying Data

A Layman's Guide to Understanding and Using Data in Everyday Life

Harlan Domer

BriteThought Publishing

BRITETHOUGHT

To my extraordinary wife,

Without your unwavering support and love throughout my career,
I would not have been able to amass the wealth of knowledge that
I am now able to share. Your belief in me has been a beacon of light
in my journey. This book is a testament to your enduring patience,
encouragement, and love.

Thank you for being my rock and my inspiration.

CONTENTS

INTRODUCTION

Greetings! Whether you're a data enthusiast or someone who finds data a tad overwhelming, fear not! I'm here to be your amiable companion on this journey through the data universe. Why should I give two hoots?

One day, I was at the grocery store, trying to decide between two brands of peanut butter. One was my usual go-to, the other was a new brand claiming to be healthier. I found myself comparing the nutritional information on the labels, and it hit me—this was data. Data isn't just numbers in a spreadsheet or statistics in a news report. It's information that helps us make decisions, big and small, every single day.

From choosing the healthiest peanut butter to deciding which route to take to work based on traffic data, we're all data users. And in this book, I'm going to show you how to become a data master.

So, buckle up, and let's dive into the exciting world of data. And don't worry, there won't be any math quizzes. I promise! (Unless you're into that sort of thing, in which case, I've got some great pie charts to show you!)

PERSONAL INTRODUCTION AND MY EXPERIENCE WITH DATA

Now, you might be wondering who I am to guide you on this data journey. Well, I'm Harlan Domer, a self-confessed data nerd with over two decades of experience in the field. I've worked with data in all its forms, from tiny data sets in small businesses to big data in multinational corporations.

I remember my first encounter with a massive data set. It was like standing at the foot of Mount Everest, equipped with nothing but a pair of flip-flops and a strong sense of optimism. But with time, patience, and a lot of coffee, I learned to navigate the data landscape. I found patterns and insights that helped businesses make informed decisions, and it was thrilling!

But enough about me. This book isn't about my love affair with data. It's about helping you understand and use data in your everyday life. So, whether you're a student, a professional, or just a curious soul, this book is for you. Let's embark on this data adventure together, shall we?

CHAPTER 1: UNDERSTANDING DATA

△△△

Welcome to the world of data! Now, before you start picturing a Matrix-like scenario with green numbers cascading down your screen, let me assure you—it's not that complex. In fact, data is something you interact with every day.

EXPLANATION OF WHAT DATA IS AND THE DIFFERENT TYPES OF DATA

Data, in its simplest form, is just information. It's the number of steps you've walked today (according to your fitness tracker), the list of movies you've watched this year (thanks, Netflix), or even the number of times you've hit the snooze button on your alarm this morning (no judgment here).

There are two main types of data: qualitative and quantitative. Qualitative data is descriptive, like the color of your eyes or your favorite ice cream flavor. Quantitative data is numerical, like your height, weight, or the number of coffee cups you consume to get through Monday (again, no judgment).

1. **Qualitative Data**: This is data that is descriptive and conceptual. It's not about numbers or quantities but about understanding and interpretation. For example, the color of your eyes, the type of music you like, or the feedback from a customer survey - these are all examples of qualitative data.

2. **Quantitative Data**: This is data that can be measured or quantified. It's all about numbers and can be used to perform statistical analysis. For example, your age, the number of steps you walked today, or the sales figures for a company - these are all examples of quantitative data.

Within these two categories, there are further types of data like nominal, ordinal, interval, and ratio data, but we'll get into those later. For now, just remember that data is everywhere, and it comes in many different forms. It's the lifeblood of decision-making and the foundation of our digital world. So, the next time you're scrolling through your social media feed or checking your bank balance, remember - you're interacting with data. Pretty cool, right?

REAL-WORLD EXAMPLES OF HOW DATA IS USED IN EVERYDAY LIFE

Now that we've defined what data is and the different types of data, let's dive into some real-world examples of how data is used in everyday life.

1. **Shopping**: Ever wondered how Amazon seems to know exactly what you need, even before you do? That's data at work. Amazon uses data from your browsing history, past purchases, and items in your cart to recommend products you might be interested in. It's like having a personal shopper who knows your taste perfectly!

2. **Entertainment**: Netflix, Spotify, and other streaming services use data to personalize your experience. They analyze your viewing or listening history to recommend movies, TV shows, or songs that you might like. So, the next time Netflix recommends a show that becomes your new favorite, you have data to thank for it!

3. **Healthcare**: Data is revolutionizing healthcare. From electronic medical records that make it easier for doctors to access your health history to wearable devices that track your heart rate and sleep patterns, data is helping us live healthier lives.

4. **Transportation**: GPS navigation systems use data to determine the fastest route to your destination, taking into account factors like traffic, road closures, and even weather conditions. Ride-sharing apps like Uber and Lyft also use data to match drivers with riders and determine pricing.

5. **Banking and Finance**: Banks use data to detect fraudulent activity. If a transaction doesn't fit your usual spending pattern, your bank will flag it as suspicious. This is why you might receive a call from your bank if you suddenly make a large purchase in a

different country.

These are just a few examples of how data is used in everyday life. The truth is data is everywhere, and it's influencing our lives in ways we might not even realize. As we continue on this journey, we'll delve deeper into the world of data and explore how we can harness its power for our benefit.

A SIMPLE EXPLANATION OF HOW DATA IS COLLECTED AND STORED

Now, let's talk about how data is collected and stored. Imagine you're at a coffee shop, and you order a latte. The barista punches in your order, which gets stored in the shop's system. That's data collection in action. Simple, right?

Data Collection

Data collection is the process of gathering information from various sources. In the digital world, every action we take generates data. When you browse a website, make an online purchase, use a mobile app, or even like a post on social media, you're creating data.

There are many ways to collect data. For example, online surveys and forms are used to collect data directly from individuals. Cookies, which are tiny files stored on your computer, collect data about your browsing habits. Mobile apps collect data about your usage and behavior within the app. Even your smart devices, like your fitness tracker or smart home devices, are collecting data about your activities and preferences.

Data Storage

But what about data storage? Well, that's a bit more complex. Your latte order, along with all the other orders, gets stored in databases. Think of a database as a giant digital filing cabinet, neatly organizing all the data for easy access. And no, it doesn't look like a scene from 'The Matrix'.

Once data is collected, it needs to be stored so that it can be accessed and analyzed later. This is where databases come in. A database is like a giant digital filing cabinet where data is organized and stored.

There are different types of databases, but the most common are relational databases. These databases organize data into tables, similar to a spreadsheet, which makes it easier to manage and retrieve.

Data can also be stored in the cloud. Cloud storage uses the internet to store data on remote servers. This allows for easy access to data from anywhere and provides a cost-effective and scalable solution for storing large amounts of data.

It's important to note that data storage must be done securely to protect the data from unauthorized access or breaches. This is a major concern in today's world, where data privacy and security are of utmost importance.

So, there you have it - a simple explanation of how data is collected and stored.

We'll dig deeper into these topics and more as we continue our journey. But for now, give yourself a pat on the back - you're well on your way to becoming a data whiz!

In the next section, we'll dive into how data impacts our daily lives. Spoiler alert: it's more than just deciding between a latte and a cappuccino.

CHAPTER 2: DATA IN THE NEWS

△△△

Welcome to Chapter 2! Now that we've got a basic understanding of what data is and how it's collected and stored let's turn our attention to a place where we encounter data on a daily basis - the news.

HOW TO UNDERSTAND DATA AND STATISTICS PRESENTED IN THE NEWS

Whether it's the latest unemployment figures, election polls, or COVID-19 statistics, data is a crucial part of news reporting. But understanding this data can sometimes feel like trying to decipher a foreign language. So, how can we make sense of it all? Let's break it down.

Understanding the Basics

First, it's important to understand the basics of the data being presented. What is the source of the data? How was it collected? What does it represent? For example, if you're looking at unemployment figures, you might want to know how unemployment is defined, how the data was collected, and what time period it covers.

Interpreting Graphs and Charts

News stories often use graphs and charts to present data. These can be a great way to visualize data, but they can also be misleading if interpreted incorrectly. Pay attention to the scale used on the graph, the units of measurement, and any labels or legends.

Understanding Percentages and Rates

Percentages and rates are commonly used in news stories to express changes in data over time or differences between groups. It's essential to understand what these percentages and rates are based on. For example, if a news story reports that unemployment has increased by 10%, you need to know whether this is a 10% increase in the number of unemployed people or a 10% increase in the unemployment rate.

Critical Thinking

Finally, it's important to apply critical thinking when interpreting data in the news. Are there any biases in the data? Are there other factors that could be influencing the results? Is the data being used to support a particular viewpoint? Remember, data is just one piece of the puzzle, and it's essential to consider the broader context.

Understanding data in the news can be challenging, but with a bit of practice and a critical eye, you'll soon be able to navigate the data landscape like a pro. So, the next time you see a graph, chart, or statistic in the news, don't just take it at face value. Dive deeper, ask questions, and make the data work for you.

COMMON WAYS DATA CAN BE MISREPRESENTED OR MISUNDERSTOOD

As we continue our journey through the world of data in the news, it's essential to understand that not all data is presented fairly or accurately. Put all political biases aside because all sides try to massage the data to tell the story they want to be heard. Sometimes, data can be misrepresented or misunderstood, either intentionally or unintentionally. Let's explore some of the common ways this can happen.

Cherry-Picking Data

Cherry-picking involves selecting data that supports a particular viewpoint while ignoring data that contradicts it. For example, a politician might highlight economic data from a specific time period that makes their policies look successful while ignoring data from other periods that are less favorable.

Misleading Graphs

Graphs can be a powerful tool for visualizing data, but they can also be used to mislead. For example, changing the scale of a graph can make differences appear larger or smaller than they really are. Pie charts can also be misleading if they don't add up to 100% or if they represent categories that overlap. Always look at the scale and add all the percentages in graphs and charts together. If percentages don't add up to 100% or are more than that, you're only getting a part of the story, or someone is trying to make something look bigger than it is.

Correlation vs. Causation

This is a common mistake in interpreting data. Just because two variables are correlated (i.e., they move together), it doesn't mean that one causes the other. For example, a news story might report that countries with higher chocolate consumption have more Nobel laureates and suggest that eating chocolate makes you smarter. In reality, these two variables are likely correlated with a third factor, like economic development, which could be the actual cause, or causation, due to a higher educational level in that country rather than anything to do with chocolate.

Ignoring Margin of Error

Election reporting is where this seems to happen the most. Almost all data comes with a margin of error, which is a measure of the uncertainty in the data. News stories often ignore this margin of error, presenting data as more precise than it really is. For example, if a poll shows one candidate leading by 2 points, but the margin of error is 3 points, the race is actually too close to call.

Overgeneralization

This happens when data from a small or non-representative sample is used to draw conclusions about a larger population. For example, a news story might report on a study that found a particular diet helped people lose weight without mentioning that the study only involved a small number of participants.

These are just a few examples of how data can be misrepresented or misunderstood in the news. Sometimes it is unintentional, but unfortunately, sometimes it is not. The key to avoiding these pitfalls is to approach data with a critical eye, ask questions, and understand the limitations of data. It has become common in our society to hear that we must "trust the numbers," but remember, although data is a powerful tool, it's not infallible. It's up to us to use and interpret it wisely.

TIPS FOR CRITICALLY EVALUATING DATA IN THE NEWS

Data in the news can be as slippery as a fish. One minute it's telling you that coffee is good for you, the next minute it's telling you it's bad, and almost anyone over 40 can tell you about the back and forth about cholesterol in food. So, how do you make sense of it all? Well, now that we've seen how data can be misrepresented or misunderstood, let's talk about how you can critically evaluate data in the news. Here are some tips to help you become a savvy data consumer.

Check the Source

The first step in assessing data is to check the source. Who collected the data? How was it collected? Is the source reputable? Remember, not all data is created equal. Data from a peer-reviewed, double-blind, scientific study is likely to be vastly more reliable than data from an online poll.

Understand the Methodology

How was the data collected and analyzed? What definitions and measurements were used? Understanding the methodology can help you assess the reliability of the data and identify any potential biases or errors.

Look for Confounding Variables

A confounding variable is a factor that can cause or prevent the outcome of interest, is not controlled by the researcher, and is associated with the element under investigation. For example, if a study finds a correlation between eating breakfast and academic performance, a confounding variable might be socioeconomic status - perhaps students who eat breakfast are also more likely to come from wealthier families, which could influence their academic performance.

Consider the Scale

When looking at graphs, pay attention to the scale. A graph can make differences appear larger or smaller depending on how the scale is set. Also, be wary of graphs that don't start at zero, as this common method is used to exaggerate differences.

Beware of Correlation vs. Causation

As we discussed earlier, just because two variables are correlated, it doesn't mean that one causes the other. Be wary of news stories that imply causation based on correlation.

Question the Interpretation

Even if the data is sound, how it is interpreted can be misleading. Be critical of the conclusions drawn from the data and consider whether other interpretations are possible.

Remember, data is a tool, not a truth serum. It can provide valuable insights, but it's not infallible. By critically evaluating data in the news, you can make more informed decisions and avoid being misled by faulty data or faulty representation of data.

FAMOUS DATA MISREPRESENTATIONS IN THE NEWS

Remember when a certain news outlet claimed that eating chocolate could help you lose weight? Turns out, they had cherry-picked data from a study that was actually designed to demonstrate how easy it is to manipulate data. The researchers behind the study were trying to make a point about the dangers of bad science, but their point got lost in the media frenzy.

Or how about the time when a major newspaper published a graph showing a strong correlation between the number of people who drowned by falling into a pool and the number of films Nicolas Cage appeared in a given year? While it's a humorous example, it's a good reminder that correlation does not imply causation.

These examples highlight the importance of critical thinking when it comes to data in the news. So, the next time you see a headline like "Eating Pizza Could Help You Live Longer", remember to take it with a grain of salt. Or in this case, a slice of pepperoni.

CHAPTER 3: BASICS OF DATA PRIVACY

ΔΔΔ

Wow, Chapter 3! You've made some significant progress in our data journey. We'll continue our journey through the world of data by tackling a topic that's becoming increasingly important in our digital age - data privacy.

OVERVIEW OF WHAT DATA PRIVACY IS AND WHY IT'S IMPORTANT

Data privacy. It sounds like something out of a spy movie, doesn't it? But it's actually a crucial part of our everyday lives. In this digital age, our personal information is more accessible than ever —and not always to the people we'd like.

What is Data Privacy?

Data privacy, also known as information privacy, is the aspect of information technology (IT) that deals with the ability of an individual or organization to determine what data in a computer system can be shared with third parties. In simple terms, it's about who has access to your data and how they can use it.

Why is Data Privacy Important?

In our digital world, we're constantly sharing data - whether we're shopping online, using social media, or even just browsing the web. This data can include everything from our names and addresses to our personal preferences and habits. While this data can be used to improve services and create a more personalized online experience, it can also be misused.

Data privacy is essential for several reasons:

1. **Personal Protection**: Without data privacy, your personal information can be misused for fraudulent activities, like identity theft.

2. **Freedom of Expression**: Data privacy allows you to express your opinions online without fear of being tracked or monitored.

3. **Business Reputation and Trust**: For businesses, data privacy is crucial for maintaining trust with customers. If a company can't protect its customers' data, it could lose their trust and their business.

4. **Legal Compliance**: Many countries have laws and regulations that require businesses to protect personal data. Failing to comply with these laws can result in hefty fines and legal consequences.

In the following sections, we'll delve deeper into the world of data privacy, exploring topics like data protection laws, data breaches, and how you can protect your own data. So, settle in and get ready for a deep dive into the world of data privacy!

EXPLANATION OF COMMON DATA PRIVACY TERMS (LIKE COOKIES, ENCRYPTION, ETC.)

As we examine the world of data privacy, it's important to familiarize ourselves with some common terms. So, let's demystify some of the jargon!

Cookies: No, we're not talking about the delicious baked goods. In the digital world, cookies are small files that are stored on your computer when you visit a website. They're used to remember information about you, like your login details or items in your shopping cart. While cookies can make your online experience more convenient, they can also be used to track your browsing habits, which raises privacy concerns.

Encryption: Encryption is a method of converting data into a code to prevent unauthorized access. It's like a secret language that can only be understood if you have the key. When data is encrypted, even if it's intercepted or stolen, it can't be read without the key.

Two-Factor Authentication (2FA) & Multi-Factor Authentication (MFA): Two-factor, and Multi-Factor, authentication is a security measure that requires two or more forms of identification to access an account or resource. This could be something you know (like a password), something you have (like a phone), or something you are (like a fingerprint). 2FA and MFA provide an extra layer of security and make it harder for unauthorized users to access your data.

Data Breach: A data breach is an incident where unauthorized individuals gain access to confidential data. This could be a hacker breaking into a company's database or an employee accidentally leaving a laptop with sensitive information in a public place.

Privacy Policy: A privacy policy is a document that explains how an organization collects, uses, and protects your personal data. It's a good idea to read the privacy policy before sharing your data with a website or app. Most organizations will have a link to their Privacy Policy on their website.

General Data Protection Regulation (GDPR): The General Data Protection Regulation (GDPR) is a law in the European Union that gives individuals control over their personal data. It requires businesses to protect the personal data of EU citizens and imposes heavy fines for data breaches.

Personal Identifiable Information (PII): PII refers to any information that can be used to identify an individual. Examples include name, social security number, address, and phone number.

Data Controller: The data controller is the entity that determines the purposes, conditions and means of the processing of personal data.

Data Processor: A data processor is the entity that processes data on behalf of the Data Controller.

Data Subject: The data subject, most likely you, is the individual whose personal data is being processed.

Data Minimization: Data minimization is a principle that states that personal data collected should be limited to what is necessary in relation to the purposes for which they are processed.

Data Protection Officer (DPO): A DPO is an enterprise security leadership role required by the General Data Protection Regulation (GDPR). DPOs oversee data protection strategy and implementation to ensure compliance with GDPR requirements.

Right to be Forgotten: This is a complex topic, also known as

Data Erasure, this right entitles the data subject to have the data controller erase their personal data, cease further dissemination of the data, and potentially have third parties halt processing of the data. This right is a significant stride towards personal data sovereignty, giving individuals control over their digital footprint.

However, it's important to note that the implementation of this right is not uniform across the globe. While it has been embraced and enforced in regions like the European Union, it is not universally available or recognized. In some jurisdictions, the right to be forgotten is still a topic of ongoing debate, often clashing with other rights such as freedom of speech and public interest.

Despite its uneven global adoption, the right to be forgotten is a powerful concept that advocates for personal privacy in an increasingly digital world. It empowers individuals to control their online presence and to dissociate themselves from data that is outdated, irrelevant, or harmful.

However, the absence of this right in certain regions highlights a significant gap in global data privacy norms. It underscores the need for international cooperation in establishing universal data privacy standards that respect individual rights.

Advocacy for the right to be forgotten is crucial. It's not just about controlling personal data, but also about shaping the future of digital rights. As we continue to navigate the digital age, the right to be forgotten will undoubtedly play a pivotal role in defining the boundaries of personal privacy and public interest.

Data Portability: This is the requirement for controllers to provide the data subject with a copy of their data in a format that allows for easy use with another controller.

Privacy by Design: Privacy by Design is an approach to systems' design which takes privacy into account throughout the whole engineering process.

Data Protection Impact Assessment (DPIA): DPIA is a process to help identify and minimize the data protection risks of a project. It is mandatory for certain types of processing, such as large scale processing of sensitive data.

Key Performance Indicator (KPI): A Key Performance Indicator, or KPI, is a measurable value demonstrating how effectively a company, department, or individual is achieving key business objectives. KPIs are used to evaluate success at reaching targets across various aspects of performance, such as sales growth, operational efficiency, customer satisfaction, and more. They provide a benchmark for progress and help guide strategic decision-making. The specific KPIs used can vary widely depending on the organization and its goals. Still, they are always tied to high-priority objectives and are critical for tracking performance over time.

These are just a few of the terms you'll come across in the world of data privacy. As we continue our journey, we'll explore these concepts in more detail and learn how they impact our digital lives.

TIPS FOR PROTECTING YOUR DATA PRIVACY ONLINE

Now that we've covered what data privacy is and some common terms, let's talk about how you can protect your data privacy online. Here are some tips:

Use Strong, Unique Passwords

Using the same password for all your online accounts is like using the same key for your house, car, and office - if one gets stolen, they all are at risk. Use a password manager to help you create and store strong, unique passwords for each of your accounts.

Enable Two-Factor & Multi-Factor Authentication

Two-factor and Multi-Factor authentication add an extra layer of security to your accounts. Even if someone gets your password, they won't be able to access your account without the second factor (like a code sent to your phone).

Be Wary of Phishing Attempts

Phishing is a type of online scam where criminals try to trick you into giving them your personal information. Be skeptical of emails or messages that ask for your personal information, especially if they create a sense of urgency.

Limit What You Share Online

The less information you share online, the less there is for someone to steal. Be mindful of what you're sharing on social media and who can see it.

Use a VPN

A Virtual Private Network (VPN) can help protect your data when you're using public Wi-Fi. It encrypts your data, making it harder for others to intercept and view it.

Regularly Check Your Privacy Settings

Many websites and apps have privacy settings that let you control who can see your information and how it's used. Regularly review these settings to make sure they're still in line with your preferences.

Read Those Privacy Policies

Before you give a website or app your personal information, read their privacy policy. This will tell you how they plan to use your data.

Remember, protecting your data privacy is an ongoing process, not a one-time task. Stay informed about the latest threats and take proactive steps to protect your data.

CHAPTER 4: USING DATA IN DECISION MAKING

ΔΔΔ

Welcome to Chapter 4! Now that we've covered the basics of data and data privacy, let's explore how data can be used to inform decision making.

EXPLANATION OF HOW DATA CAN INFORM DECISION MAKING

What is Data-Driven Decision Making?

Data-driven decision making (DDDM) is a process that involves collecting data based on measurable goals or KPIs, analyzing patterns and facts from these insights, and utilizing them to develop strategies and activities that benefit the business in several areas.

Why Use Data in Decision Making?

Data provides a solid foundation for decision making. Instead of relying on gut feelings or assumptions, decision makers can use data to understand trends, identify opportunities and challenges, and predict outcomes. This can lead to more confident decisions and better results.

How to Use Data in Decision Making

1. **Define Your Goals**: Before you can use data to make decisions, you need to know what you're trying to achieve. Your goals will guide your data collection and analysis.

2. **Collect Relevant Data**: Once you've defined your goals, you need to collect data that can help you achieve them. This might involve collecting new data or using data you already have.

3. **Analyze the Data**: After collecting data, you need to analyze it to find patterns and insights. This might involve statistical analysis, data visualization, or data mining.

4. **Make Decisions Based on the Data**: Finally, you can use the insights from your data analysis to make informed decisions. This might involve choosing a course of action, setting a strategy, or making a prediction about the future.

5. **Review and Refine**: Data-driven decision making isn't a one-time process. Once you've made a decision, you can collect more data to see how well it's working and make adjustments as needed.

In the following sections, we'll delve deeper into each of these steps and explore how you can use data to make better decisions in your personal and professional life.

Examples of How to Use Data in Personal Decisions (Like Health, Finance, Etc.)

Let's now look at some examples of how data can be used to inform personal decisions, particularly in areas like health and finance.

Health Decisions

With the advent of wearable technology and health apps, collecting data about your health is easier than ever. For example, you might use a fitness tracker to collect data about your physical activity, sleep patterns, and heart rate. This data can help you understand your health habits and make informed decisions about things like diet and exercise. For instance, if your data shows you're not getting enough sleep, you might decide to adjust your bedtime or morning routine.

Financial Decisions

Data can also play a big role in personal finance. Many banks and financial apps provide data about your spending habits, which can help you understand where your money is going and make decisions about budgeting and saving. For example, if your data shows you're spending a lot of money on dining out, you might decide to cook at home more often to save money.

Travel Decisions

When planning a trip, you can use data to decide when to travel, where to stay, and what to do. For example, you might use data about flight prices to decide the best time to book a flight or data about hotel ratings and prices to choose a place to stay.

Shopping Decisions

Online shopping platforms often provide data about products, such as customer reviews and ratings, which can help you make informed decisions about what to buy. For example, if you're deciding between two products, you might choose the one with higher customer ratings.

Remember, the key to using data in personal decision making is to collect relevant data, analyze it to find insights, and then use those insights to make informed decisions.

INTRODUCTION TO SIMPLE DATA ANALYSIS TECHNIQUES

Now that we've seen how data can be used in personal decisions, let's introduce some simple data analysis techniques that you can use to make sense of your data.

Descriptive Statistics

Descriptive statistics provide a summary of your data. They include measures like mean (average), median (middle value), mode (most common value), and range (difference between the highest and lowest values). These measures can give you a general understanding of your data.

Data Visualization

Data visualization involves creating graphical representations of your data. This can include bar graphs, pie charts, line graphs, and scatter plots. Visualizing your data can make it easier to understand and can reveal patterns or trends that might not be obvious from the raw data.

Correlation Analysis

Correlation analysis is used to understand the relationship between two variables. For example, you might use correlation analysis to see if there's a relationship between the amount of exercise you get and your sleep quality.

Regression Analysis

Regression analysis is a more advanced technique that allows you to predict one variable based on the value of another. For example, you might use regression analysis to predict your future weight based on your current diet and exercise habits.

Hypothesis Testing

Hypothesis testing is a statistical method used to make decisions or draw conclusions about a population based on sample data. For example, you might use hypothesis testing to decide if a change in your diet has resulted in weight loss.

Remember, these are just a few of the many data analysis techniques available. The best technique to use depends on the data and what you're trying to understand or achieve.

CHAPTER 5: FUTURE OF DATA
EMERGING TECHNOLOGIES: CLOUD PLATFORMS

Before we dive into the ocean of emerging trends in data, let's take a moment to talk about a technology that's already making waves: Cloud Platforms. Imagine storing all your stuff in an invisible, magical cloud that follows you everywhere. Need a file? Just reach into the cloud. Want to run a program? The cloud's got your back. That's what Cloud Platforms are like, but for data and applications.

There are several big players in the Cloud Platform game, and we will talk about three of them: AWS, Azure, and Google Cloud.

1. **AWS (Amazon Web Services)**: Picture a massive, bustling city that never sleeps. That's AWS. It's part of Amazon, the same company that delivers your favorite books and gadgets right to your doorstep. But instead of delivering packages, AWS delivers over 200 different services, including storage, computing power, and databases. It's like a one-stop-shop for all your cloud needs. For example, if you're a photographer, you could use AWS to store all your high-resolution photos. Or if you're a business owner, you could use AWS to host your website and manage your customer data.

2. **Azure**: Now, imagine a Swiss Army knife. It's got a tool for every situation, right? That's Azure in a nutshell. Microsoft's cloud platform offers a wide range of services from data storage to

machine learning. And because it's from Microsoft, it plays really well with other Microsoft products like Office 365 and Outlook. So, if you're a student, you could use Azure to store and share your school projects. Or if you're a scientist, you could use Azure's machine-learning tools to analyze your research data.

3. **Google Cloud**: Finally, think of the most intelligent person you know. They always seem to have an answer for everything, don't they? That's what Google Cloud is like. It's Google's cloud platform, known for its powerful data analytics and machine learning capabilities. It's like having a super-smart assistant who can help you make sense of your data. For example, if you're a small business owner, you could use Google Cloud to analyze your sales data and find out which products are most popular. Or if you're a city planner, you could use Google Cloud to analyze traffic data and improve city infrastructure.

These Cloud Platforms are changing the way we store and use data, making it more accessible and flexible than ever before. They're like the superheroes of the data world, each with their own unique powers. Now, let's dive deeper into the ocean of data trends...

.

Discussion of Emerging Trends in Data (Like Big Data, AI, Etc.)

Data is at the forefront of many emerging trends in the rapidly evolving world of technology. As we look toward the future, several key developments are shaping the data landscape and how we interact with it.

1. **Adaptive AI Systems**: Imagine if your GPS could learn from your driving habits and adapt its directions accordingly. That's what Adaptive AI Systems do. They're like super-smart GPS

systems that can quickly adjust to changes, making decisions faster and more flexible. So, if there's a sudden roadblock, it can quickly find a new route. This makes it different from Data-centric AI, which focuses more on the quality of data going into the system, while Adaptive AI is all about how the system responds and adapts to changes.

2. **Data-centric AI**: Think of Data-centric AI as a super-smart robot chef. To make a great meal, it needs the right ingredients—that's where data comes in. Just like our chef needs fresh veggies and spices, AI needs good-quality data to work well. If we give it the wrong data (like rotten tomatoes or too much salt), it can make mistakes—big ones. That's why it's super important to ensure our AI gets the best data we can give it. This means we need to check our data for things like bias (making sure it's fair), diversity (making sure it's varied), and labeling (making sure it's organized). This is called a data-centric AI approach—it's all about focusing on the data to make our AI the best chef it can be!

3. **Metadata-driven Data Fabric**: Imagine if your clothes could learn about you and adapt to your needs. Your sweater could cool you down when it's hot, or your shoes could become more comfortable after a long day. That's kind of what a Metadata-driven Data Fabric does but with data instead of clothes. It learns from the information it has (the metadata) and uses that to make decisions and suggestions. This helps people and systems trust and use the data better. It's like having an intelligent wardrobe for your data!

4. **Always Share Data**: Data sharing is a critical digital transformation capability. To promote data sharing and increase access to the right data aligned to the business case it's important to collaborate across business and industry lines.

5. **Context-enriched Analysis**: Imagine you're trying to solve a puzzle, but you're not sure where each piece goes. Context-enriched analysis is like a friend who helps you figure it out. It

looks at each puzzle piece (or piece of data), finds clues about where it might go (like color or shape), and then helps you put it in the right place. It's a way of understanding data better by looking at how it's connected and what it has in common with other data. It's like having a puzzle-solving buddy for your data!

6. **Business-composed Data and Analytics**: This trend focuses on the people side, shifting from IT to business. It enables business users or technologists to craft business-driven data and analytics capabilities collaboratively.

7. **Decision-centric Data and Analytics**: The discipline of decision intelligence is causing organizations to rethink their investments in data and analytics capabilities. Use decision intelligence disciplines to design the best decision and then deliver the required inputs.

8. **Skills and Literacy Shortfall**: Skills and Literacy Shortfall: Understanding data is becoming as important as reading and writing. But right now, not enough people have these skills. By 2025, most Chief Data Officers (CDOs)—the people in charge of a company's data strategy—will struggle to teach their teams the data skills they need to meet their business goals. It's like trying to read a book but not knowing the alphabet. We need to get better at teaching data literacy.

9. **Connected Governance**: Organizations need effective governance at all levels that not only addresses their existing operational challenges, but is also flexible, scalable, and highly responsive to changing market dynamics and strategic organizational challenges.

10. **AI Risk Management**: Organizations that develop trustworthy, purpose-driven AI will see over 75% of AI innovations succeed, compared to 40% among those that don't.

Now, you might be scratching your head and thinking, "Wait

a minute, those percentages don't add up to 100%!" That's on purpose, and you are right. This is a perfect example of why understanding data and how it's presented is so important, a lesson we've been emphasizing throughout this book.

You see, the percentages here aren't meant to add up to 100% because they're not parts of a whole. Instead, they're comparing the success rates of AI innovations in two different types of organizations: those that develop trustworthy, purpose-driven AI and those that don't.

So, when we say that over 75% of AI innovations succeed in organizations that develop trustworthy, purpose-driven AI, we mean that three out of every four AI projects in these organizations are successful. On the other hand, in organizations that don't prioritize trust and purpose in their AI development, only two out of every five AI projects succeed.

This is a crucial distinction to understand. It's not about adding up to a certain total, but about comparing different success rates. It's like comparing the batting averages of two baseball players. One player might hit the ball 75% of the time, while another player might only hit it 40% of the time. The percentages don't add up to 100%, but they tell us who's more likely to hit the ball.

So, remember, data can be tricky. It's not always about adding up to 100%. Sometimes, it's about understanding what the numbers are really telling us. And that's a lesson worth remembering, whether you're dealing with AI innovations or baseball statistics.

.11. **Vendor and Region Ecosystems**: Regional data security laws are making many global organizations build regional data and analytics ecosystems to comply with local regulations.

12. **Expansion to the Edge**: More data and analytics activities are executed in distributed devices, servers, or gateways located outside data centers and public cloud infrastructure. They

increasingly reside in edge computing environments, closer to where the data and decisions of interest are created and executed.

HOW THESE TRENDS MIGHT IMPACT EVERYDAY LIFE

As we consider the impact of these emerging data trends on everyday life, it's clear that the changes will be profound and far-reaching.

1. **Adaptive AI Systems**: These systems could make our digital assistants more responsive and intuitive, adapting to our routines and preferences for a more personalized experience.

2. **Data-centric AI**: This could lead to more accurate and reliable AI systems, from recommendation algorithms on shopping sites to diagnostic tools in healthcare.

3. **Metadata-driven Data Fabric**: This could improve the way we search for and access information online, making it easier to find relevant and trustworthy content.

4. **Always Share Data**: Increased data sharing could lead to more collaborative and innovative solutions to global challenges, from climate change to public health crises.

5. **Context-enriched Analysis**: This could enhance our online experiences, from more relevant search results to more personalized content recommendations.

6. **Business-composed Data and Analytics**: This could empower more people to make data-driven decisions in their work, leading to more efficient and effective organizations.

7. **Decision-centric Data and Analytics**: This could lead to more informed and effective decision-making in all areas of life, from business strategy to personal finance.

8. **Skills and Literacy Shortfall**: The need for data literacy could

influence education and job training programs, leading to more emphasis on these skills in schools and workplaces.

9. **Connected Governance**: This could lead to more transparent and accountable organizations, as data governance practices make tracking and understanding their activities easier.

10. **AI Risk Management**: Trustworthy, purpose-driven AI could lead to more ethical and responsible use of technology, reducing the risk of harmful consequences.

11. **Vendor and Region Ecosystems**: This could impact the way we use online services, as companies adapt their practices to comply with regional data laws.

12. **Expansion to the Edge**: This could lead to faster and more reliable online services, as data processing moves closer to the source.

Importance of Data Literacy in The Future

As we look towards the future, one thing becomes increasingly clear: data literacy will be crucial. But why is it so important?

Understanding the World Around Us

In the digital age, data is everywhere. It's used to make decisions, solve problems, and understand the world around us. Without data literacy, we risk being left behind, unable to understand or contribute to the data-driven conversations that are shaping our society.

Making Informed Decisions

Data literacy is not just about understanding data, but also about using it to make informed decisions. Whether it's deciding which product to buy, which political candidate to support, or which health advice to follow, data can provide valuable insights. But without data literacy, we might not be able to interpret this data correctly, leading to poor decisions.

Protecting Our Privacy

As more of our personal information becomes digitized, understanding data becomes crucial for protecting our privacy. Data literacy can help us understand what information is being collected about us, how it's being used, and how we can protect ourselves.

Career Opportunities

In the job market, data literacy is becoming increasingly valuable. Many jobs now require some level of data literacy, and this growing trend will likely continue. By developing data literacy skills, individuals can open up a wide range of career opportunities.

Contributing to Society

Finally, data literacy is important for contributing to society. Many of the world's most pressing problems, from climate change to public health, are data problems at heart. By understanding data, we can contribute to the solutions to these problems.

In conclusion, data literacy is not just a nice-to-have skill for the future - it's a must-have. As the world becomes increasingly data-driven, we must develop our data literacy skills to keep up.

CONCLUSION

Well done, and thank you! You have made it through this book. I am sure some parts were more interesting to you than others, but it is paramount to understand as many aspects of the modern data landscape as possible, and you've taken a great leap towards that understanding, so I say again. Well done!

RECAP OF MAIN POINTS

As we wrap up this journey through the world of data, let's take a moment to recap the main points we've covered:

1. **Understanding Data**: We started with the basics, explaining what data is and the different types of data. We also looked at real-world examples of how data is used in everyday life and discussed how data is collected and stored.

2. **Data in the News**: We then explored how to understand data and statistics presented in the news, including common ways data can be misrepresented or misunderstood, and tips for critically evaluating data in the news.

3. **Basics of Data Privacy**: We explored the important topic of data privacy, explaining what it is, why it's important, and common data privacy terms. We also provided tips for protecting your data privacy online.

4. **Using Data in Decision Making**: We discussed how data can inform decision making, providing examples of how to use data in personal decisions and introducing simple data analysis techniques.

5. **Future of Data**: Finally, we looked to the future, discussing emerging trends in data and how these trends might impact everyday life. We also emphasized the importance of data literacy in the future.

Throughout this book, we've seen that data is not just a collection of numbers or facts, but a powerful tool that can inform decisions, shape our understanding of the world, and even influence the future.

ENCOURAGEMENT FOR CONTINUED LEARNING

As we close this book, I want to leave you with a final thought: the journey of learning about data doesn't end here. In fact, it's just beginning.

Data is a vast and ever-evolving field, with new developments and discoveries happening all the time. The more you learn about data, the more you'll realize how much there is to know. But don't be daunted. Each new piece of knowledge is a step forward, a new tool in your toolkit, a new lens through which to view the world.

So, I encourage you to keep learning. Keep asking questions. Keep exploring. Whether it's diving deeper into a topic we've covered in this book, or branching out into a new area of data, there's always more to discover.

Remember, in the world of data, curiosity isn't just a trait, it's a superpower. So, stay curious, keep learning, and who knows where your data journey will take you next.

GLOSSARY

Not all of the following terms appeared in this book, but you may likely come across them on your data journey. So here they are for your reference.

Alpha Level: The probability of rejecting the null hypothesis when it is true.

ANOVA (Analysis of Variance): A statistical method used to test differences between two or more means.

Bias: The systematic error introduced into sampling or testing by selecting or encouraging one outcome or answer over others.

Binomial Distribution: A probability distribution that summarizes the likelihood that a value will take one of two independent values.

Confidence Level: The percentage of all possible samples that can be expected to include the true population parameter.

Covariance: A measure of how much two random variables vary together.

Data Mining: The process of discovering patterns and knowledge from large amounts of data.

Factor Analysis: A statistical method used to describe variability among observed, correlated variables in terms of a potentially lower number of unobserved variables called factors.

Heteroscedasticity: A situation in which the variability of a variable is unequal across the range of values of a second variable that predicts it.

Monte Carlo Simulation: A computerized mathematical technique that allows people to account for risk in quantitative analysis and decision making.

ADDITIONAL RESOURCES

These additional resources are tools for you to use to help dissect and understand the data you are presented with.

Mean: The average of a set of numbers. It's calculated by adding all the numbers and then dividing by the number of numbers.

Example: If you have the numbers 1, 2, and 3, the mean would be $(1+2+3)/3 = 2$.

Median: The middle number in a set of numbers. If the set has an even number of observations, the median is the average of the two middle numbers.

Example: In the set 1, 2, 3, 4, the median is $(2+3)/2 = 2.5$.

Mode: The number that appears most frequently in a data set.

Example: In the set 1, 2, 2, 3, the mode is 2.

Range: The difference between the highest and lowest numbers in a data set.

Example: In the set 1, 2, 3, 4, the range is $4-1 = 3$.

Standard Deviation: A measure of the amount of variation or dispersion of a set of values.

Example: For the set 1, 2, 3, 4, the standard deviation can be calculated as follows:

First, calculate the mean (average): $(1+2+3+4)/4 = 2.5$
Then, subtract the mean from each number and square the result: $(1-2.5)^2 = 2.25$, $(2-2.5)^2 = 0.25$, $(3-2.5)^2 = 0.25$, $(4-2.5)^2 = 2.25$
Next, calculate the mean of these squared differences: $(2.25+0.25+0.25+2.25)/4 = 1.25$
Finally, take the square root of this number: $\sqrt{1.25} = 1.12$. This is the standard deviation.

ABOUT THE AUTHOR

Harlan Domer

Meet Harlan, a man of many hats. A data whisperer, an outdoor enthusiast, a science lover, a family man, and a leader with a heart. Harlan's life is a vibrant mosaic of diverse interests, with science being the central piece that brings it all together.

Harlan's journey with data began as a childhood fascination and evolved into a successful career. But Harlan is not just about crunching numbers. He's a seasoned leader with a knack for steering the ship, whether it's navigating the complex world of business or sailing on the open seas. His management skills are as impressive as his data expertise, making him a force to be reckoned with in the boardroom and beyond.

Away from the world of data and leadership, Harlan is an adventurer at heart. He loves hiking through the wilderness, sailing upon the vast oceans, and casting a line in serene lakes. His love for the outdoors is only matched by his love for science, a testament to his insatiable curiosity and thirst for knowledge.

Family and travel are two of Harlan's greatest joys. He cherishes the time spent with his loved ones and the memories made in far-flung corners of the world. His travels not only feed his adventurous spirit but also enrich his understanding of data, providing fresh perspectives and insights.

Harlan is a firm believer in nurturing creativity, whether it's in the realm of art and philosophy or dabbled throughout the canvas of life. He's known for his approachable demeanor, infectious enthusiasm, and ability to simplify complex concepts, making him a go-to figure in the data community and beyond.

And while Harlan's life is full of diverse passions and pursuits, there's a subtle thread that weaves through his journey, guiding him like a compass; never to be dissuaded from his ultimate goals.

So, buckle up and get ready for a fun and enlightening journey into the world of data with Harlan. It's not just about numbers and statistics; it's about life, adventure, leadership, and the endless possibilities that life brings.

www.ingramcontent.com/pod-product-compliance
Lightning Source LLC
Chambersburg PA
CBHW071118260726
48661CB00006B/2634